newton fault
rebuilt by humans

Wise Publications
part of The Music Sales Group

London / New York / Paris / Sydney / Copenhagen / Berlin / Madrid / Tokyo

Published by
Wise Publications
14-15 Berners Street, London, W1T 3LJ, UK.

Exclusive distributors:
Music Sales Limited
Distribution Centre, Newmarket Road,
Bury St Edmunds, Suffolk, IP33 3YB, UK.

Music Sales Pty Limited
20 Resolution Drive, Caringbah, NSW 2229, Australia.

Order No. AM998910   ISBN 978-1-84938-297-7

Edited by Tom Farncombe.
Music arranged by Arthur Dick.
Music processed by Paul Ewers Music Design.
Art direction & design by Steve Stacey.
Photography by Justin Aitken.
Printed in the EU.

Special thanks to Matt Buchanan for his help with proof-reading and editing the arrangements,
and to Nick Benjamin for his insights into Newton Faulkner's guitar set-ups.

www.musicsales.com

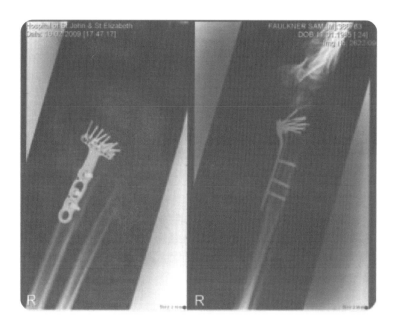

So, here we are again: album two! The 'difficult second album' made slightly more difficult by breaking my wrist five days before I was meant to start recording. I say break, but actually I just fractured my radius and dislocated my whole right hand. Anyway, it's all fine now. You can probably tell which tracks I wrote with the splint still on though…

I guess I should apologise for the amount of different tunings on this one. Just to make it a bit more complicated, I also used a baritone guitar for one track, which is just plain selfish and very un-inclusive, but it's arranged here so you can play it on a regular guitar.

All that said, I hope you enjoy playing these songs – and manage to avoid damaging yourself or your instrument in the process of learning it!

Newton Faulkner, 2009

guitar tablature explained

Guitar music can be notated in three different ways: on a musical stave, in tablature, and in rhythm slashes.

RHYTHM SLASHES: are written above the stave. Strum chords in the rhythm indicated. Round noteheads indicate single notes.

THE MUSICAL STAVE: shows pitches and rhythms and is divided by lines into bars. Pitches are named after the first seven letters of the alphabet.

TABLATURE: graphically represents the guitar fingerboard. Each horizontal line represents a string, and each number represents a fret.

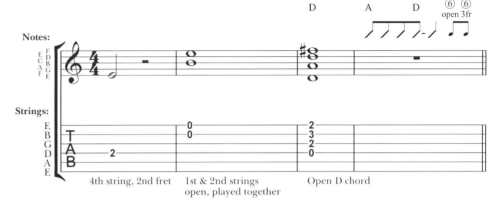

4th string, 2nd fret | 1st & 2nd strings open, played together | Open D chord

definitions for special guitar notation

SEMI-TONE BEND: Strike the note and bend up a semi-tone (½ step).

WHOLE-TONE BEND: Strike the note and bend up a whole-tone (full step).

GRACE NOTE BEND: Strike the note and bend as indicated. Play the first note as quickly as possible.

QUARTER-TONE BEND: Strike the note and bend up a ¼ step

BEND & RELEASE: Strike the note and bend up as indicated, then release back to the original note.

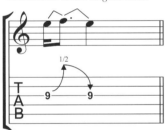

COMPOUND BEND & RELEASE: Strike the note and bend up and down in the rhythm indicated.

PRE-BEND: Bend the note as indicated, then strike it.

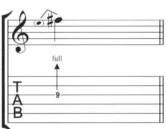

PRE-BEND & RELEASE: Bend the note as indicated. Strike it and release the note back to the original pitch.

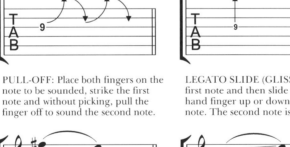

HAMMER-ON: Strike the first note with one finger, then sound the second note (on the same string) with another finger by fretting it without picking.

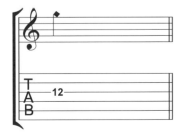

PULL-OFF: Place both fingers on the note to be sounded, strike the first note and without picking, pull the finger off to sound the second note.

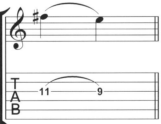

LEGATO SLIDE (GLISS): Strike the first note and then slide the same fret-hand finger up or down to the second note. The second note is not struck.

SHIFT SLIDE (GLISS & RESTRIKE): Same as legato slide, except the second note is struck.

NATURAL HARMONIC: Strike the note while the fret-hand lightly touches the string directly over the fret indicated.

TAP HARMONIC: The note is fretted normally and a harmonic is produced by 'slapping' or tapping the fret indicated in brackets (which will be twelve frets higher than the fretted note.)

PALM MUTING: The note is partially muted by the pick hand lightly touching the string(s) just before the bridge.

MUFFLED STRINGS: A percussive sound is produced by laying the first hand across the string(s) without depressing, and striking them with the pick hand.

6

TRILL: Very rapidly alternate between the notes indicated by continuously hammering-on and pulling-off.

TAPPING: Hammer ('tap') the fret indicated with the pick-hand index or middle finger and pull-off to the note fretted by the fret hand.

FINGER PICKING: Traditional notation for picking. p = thumb; i = first (index finger); m = middle finger; a = ring finger.

ARPEGGIATE: Play the notes of the chord indicated by quickly rolling them from bottom to top.

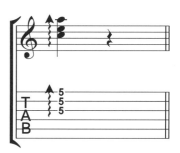

special percussive techniques

BASS THUMP: Strike body of guitar below sound-hole with the heel of the hand to create a deep, kick drum style thump.

HAMMER-ON 'FROM NOWHERE': Strike note on fretboard with fretting hand (i.e., without picking the string with the other hand).

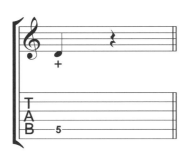

Strike with fingers below sound-hole.

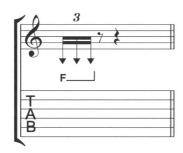

Hit on side of the body of the guitar with left (fretting) hand to create a sharp, high sound (the 'snare' response to the 'kick drum' effect on the left).

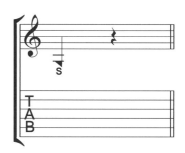

additional musical definitions

 (accent) Accentuate note (play it louder)

D.S. al Coda   Go back to the sign (𝄋), then play until the bar marked **To Coda** ⊕ then skip to the section marked ⊕ **Coda**

 (accent) Accentuate note with greater intensity

D.C. al Fine   Go back to the beginning of the song and play until the bar marked **Fine.**

(staccato) Shorten time value of note

tacet   Instrument is silent (drops out).

⊓   Downstroke

∨   Upstroke

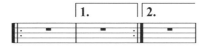 Repeat bars between signs

NOTE: Tablature numbers in brackets mean:
1. The note is sustained, but a new articulation (such as hammer on or slide) begins
2. A note may be fretted but not necessarily played.

When a repeat section has different endings, play the first ending only the first time and the second ending only the second time.

additional information

Newton Faulkner's main guitars for live use are a pair of JOM (Jumbo Orchestral Model) instruments made by Nick Benjamin:

1) A JOM model in Sitka Spruce and Mahogany with an LR Baggs Double-Barrel pickup system. This system uses an undersaddle pickup in the bridge, and an additional microphone inside the body of the guitar. This enables the various percussive effects to be heard live.

2) A similar model, set up identically, but with an Adirondack Spruce top.

Both of these guitars have been fitted with a replaceable spruce scratchplate on the lower side of the guitar front, to facilitate percussive hits and scratches while protecting the instrument from damage. This is visible in the picture below.

On stage, these guitars are run through a digital EQ unit, which allows for rapid selection of preset EQ settings when guitars are changed over between songs. Newton now uses in-ear monitors, which reduce the potential for feedback problems traditionally experienced with amplified acoustic instruments and standard foldback.

In addition to these instruments, and other Benjamin models, Newton has also started using a Baritone guitar (pictured). This has a longer, 700mm scale length and features the distinctive 'Benjamin Scoop' cutaway for upper fret access. This instrument is constructed from Honduras Rosewood, with a Lutz spruce top, and is fitted with an LR Baggs iMix pickup system. The guitar is set up to easily allow for tunings as low as 'B' or 'A' below a standard guitar. This is heard on the track 'First Time', where the 6th string is tuned right down to $A^\flat$(!). This song is arranged in this book to be played on standard guitar, sounding an octave higher than the original.

For further information about Benjamin guitars, please visit www.benjaminguitars.co.uk. There is currently a waiting time of approx. 3 years for new Benjamin guitars, so please bear this in mind when making enquiries!

Intro (interlude)

Music by Newton Faulkner

Tuning
6 = D 3 = G
5 = G 2 = A
4 = D 1 = D

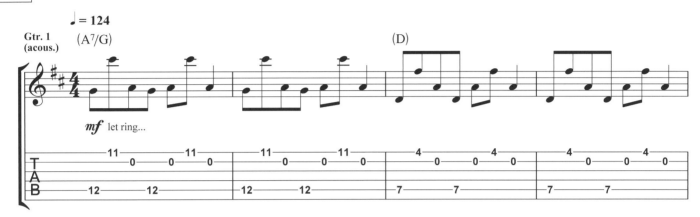

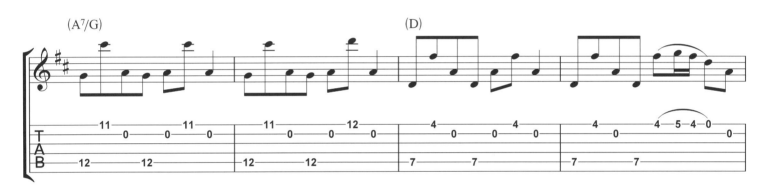

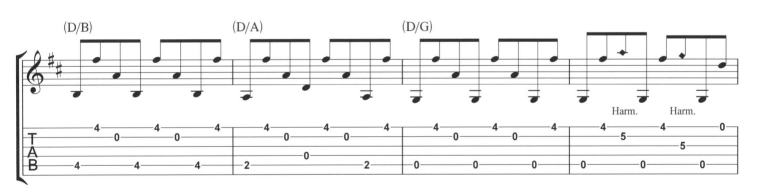

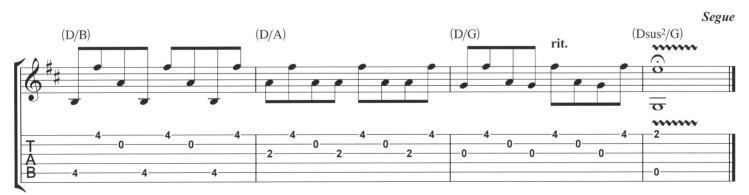

badman

Words & Music by Newton Faulkner & Toby Faulkner

Percussive notation:
H = strike body of guitar above sound-hole with heel of the hand
+ = Fretting hand hammer-on 'from nowhere'

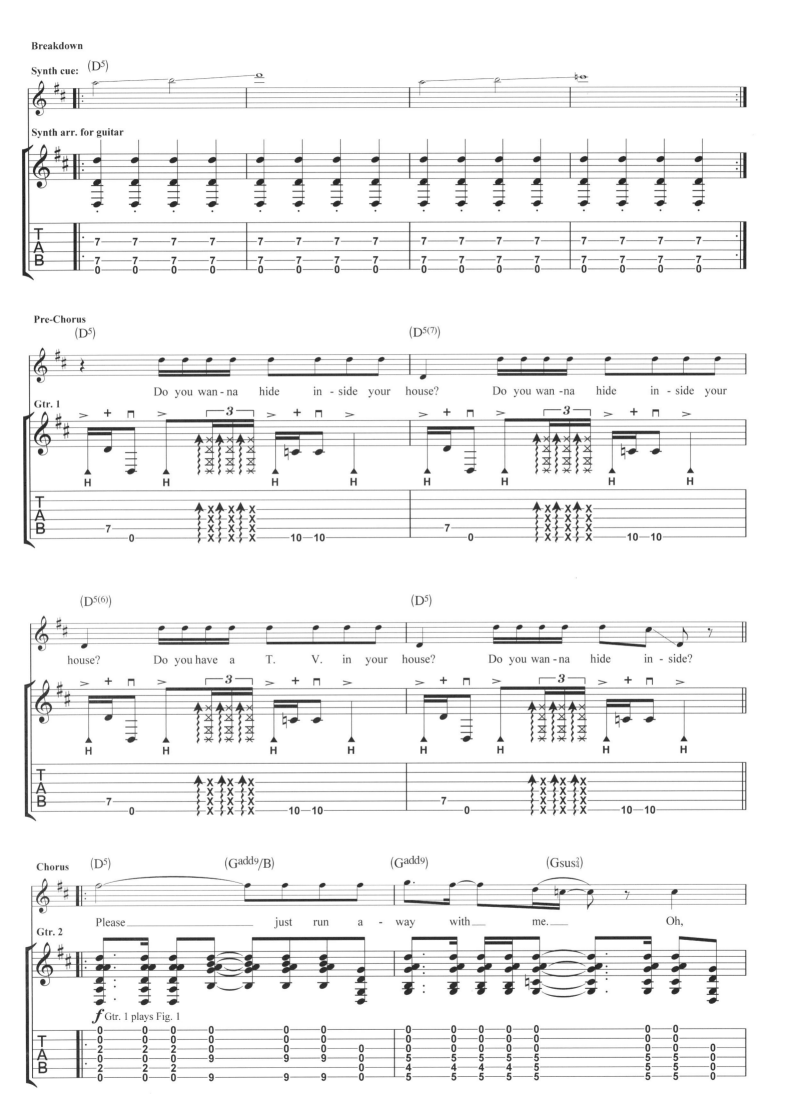

14

i took it out on you

Words & Music by Newton Faulkner & Toby Faulkner

Tuning	
6 = D	3 = F#
5 = G	2 = A
4 = D	1 = D

To match the recording, tune guitar down a further semitone

Intro ♩ = 120

Gtr. 1 (acous.)

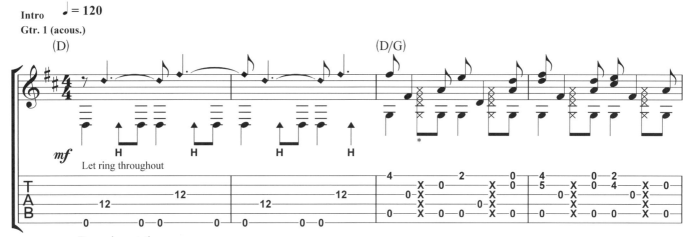

mf

Let ring throughout

Percussive notation:
H = strike body of guitar above sound hole with heel of the hand   *L.H. mute/percussive R.H. stroke

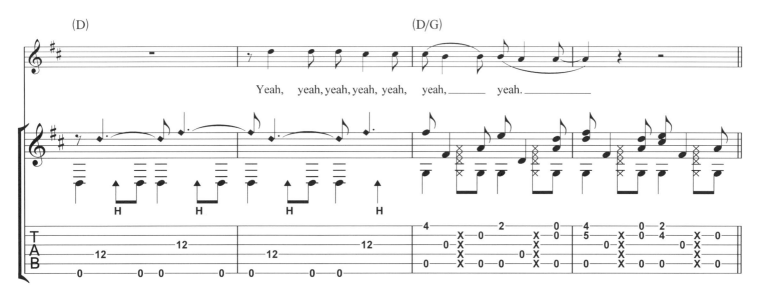

Yeah,   yeah, yeah, yeah, yeah,   yeah,_____ yeah._____

Verse

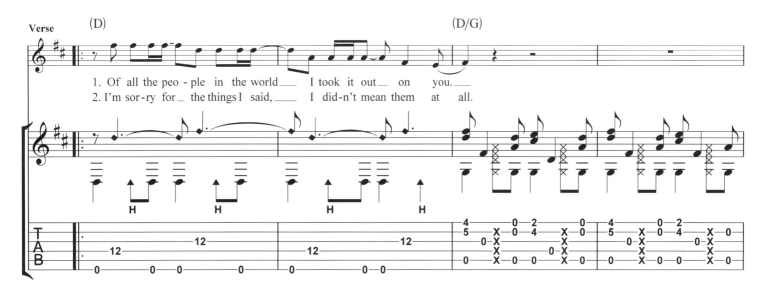

1. Of all the peo - ple in the world____ I took it out____ on   you.____
2. I'm sor - ry for _ the things I said,____ I did-n't mean them   at   all.

16

*strum including open strings & let ring...

*fill out rhythm around accents *ad lib.*

18

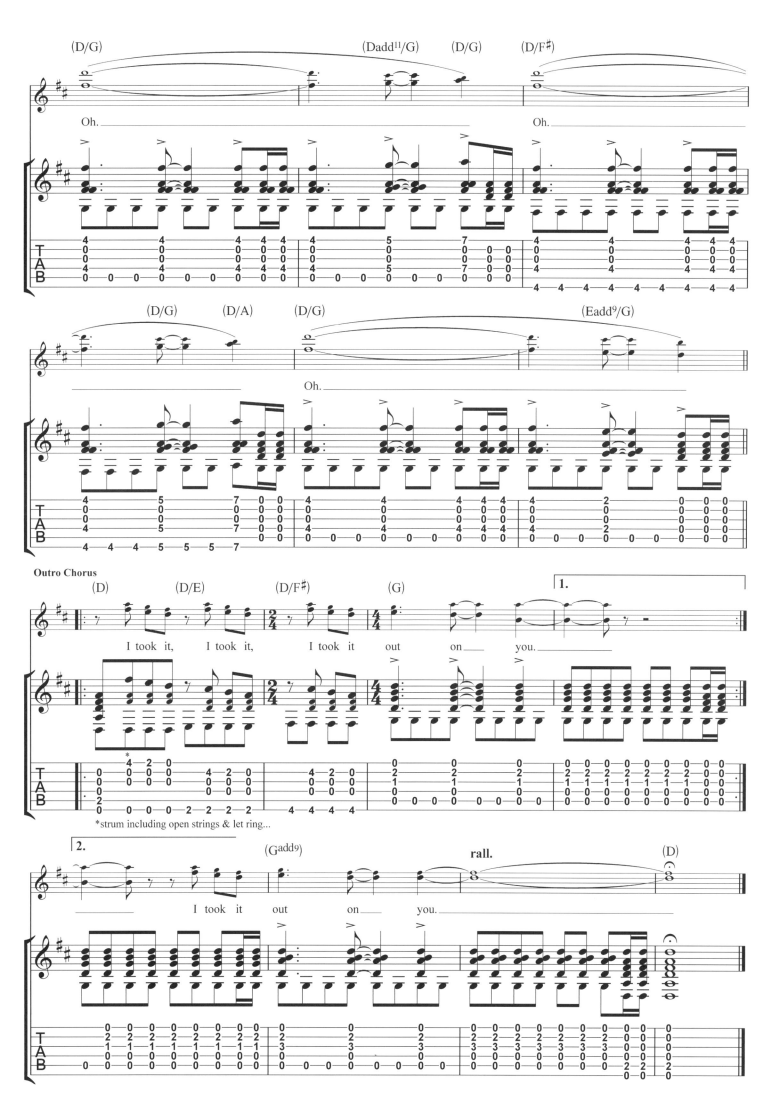

hello (interlude)

Music by Newton Faulkner & Toby Faulkner

Tuning
6 = E   3 = G
5 = A   2 = B
4 = D   1 = E

To match the recording, use a capo, 1st fret

♩ = 148

Gtr. 1 (acous. - guitarlele)

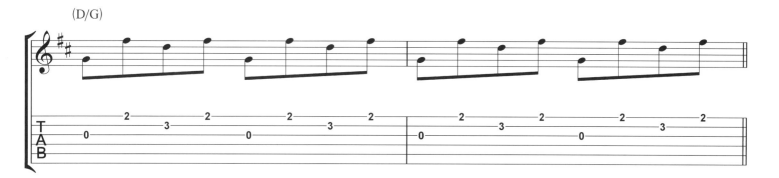

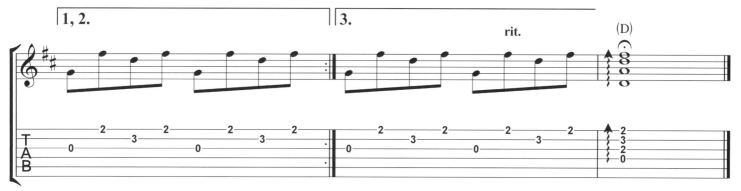

if this is it

Words & Music by Newton Faulkner & Adam Argyle

Percussive notation:
H = strike body of guitar above sound-hole with heel of the hand
S = L.H. hit on lower left side of guitar

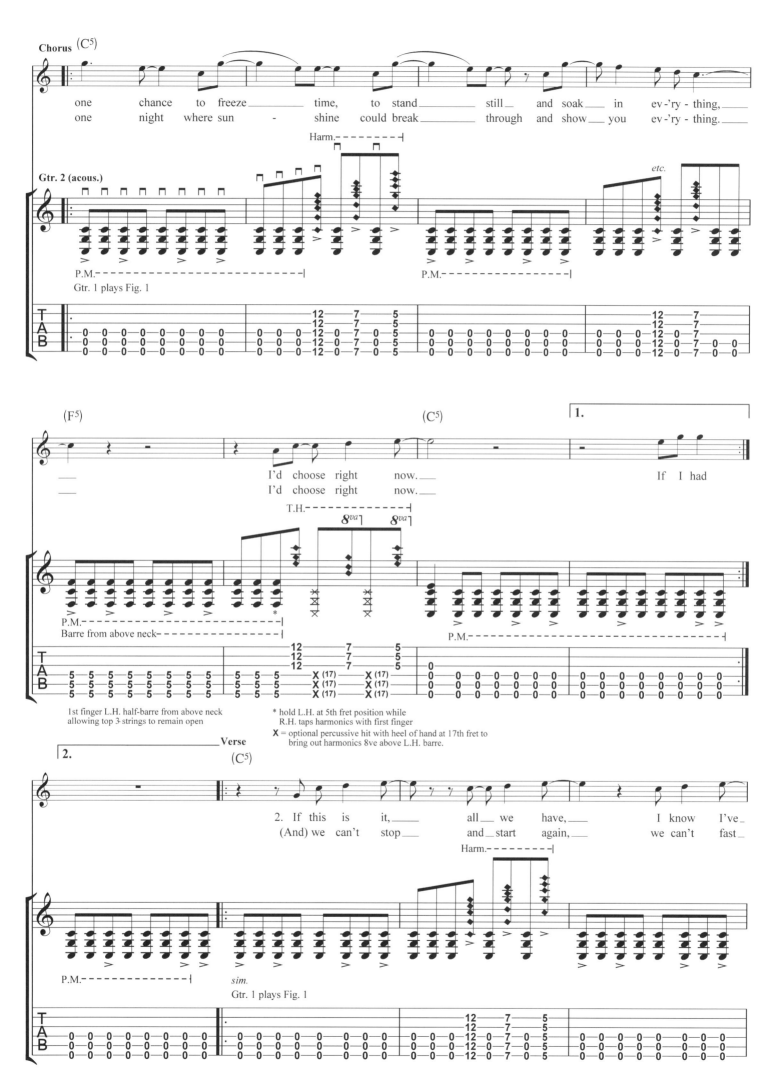

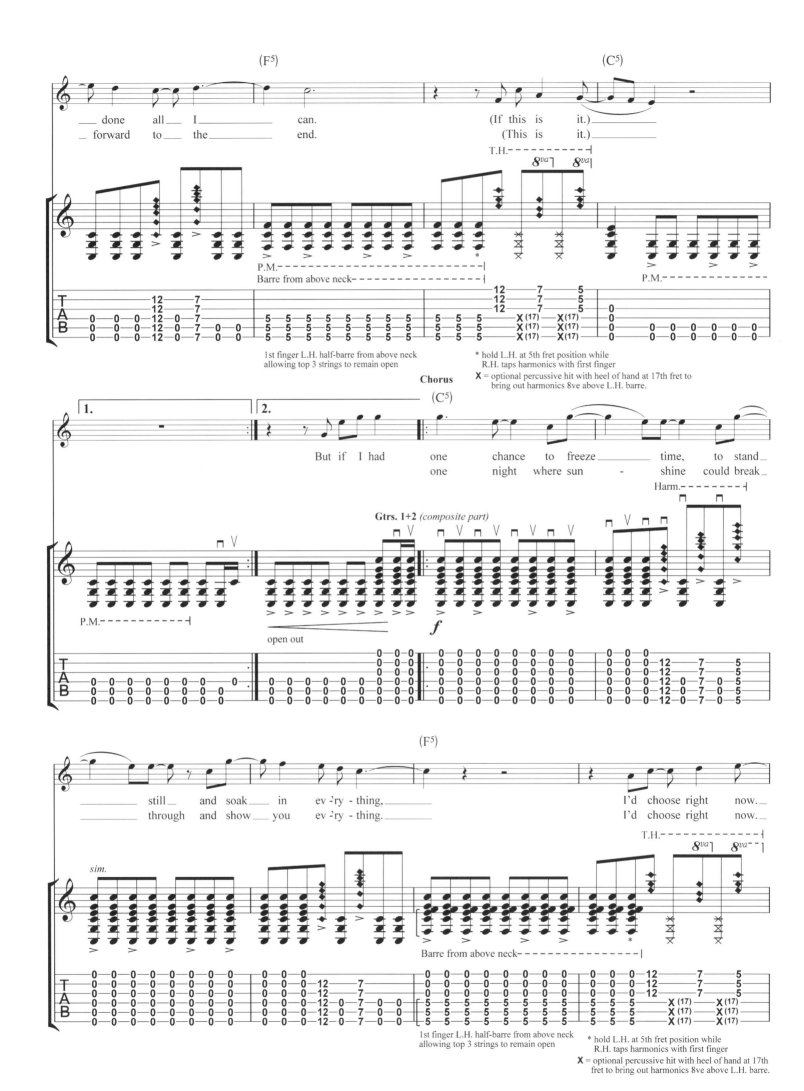

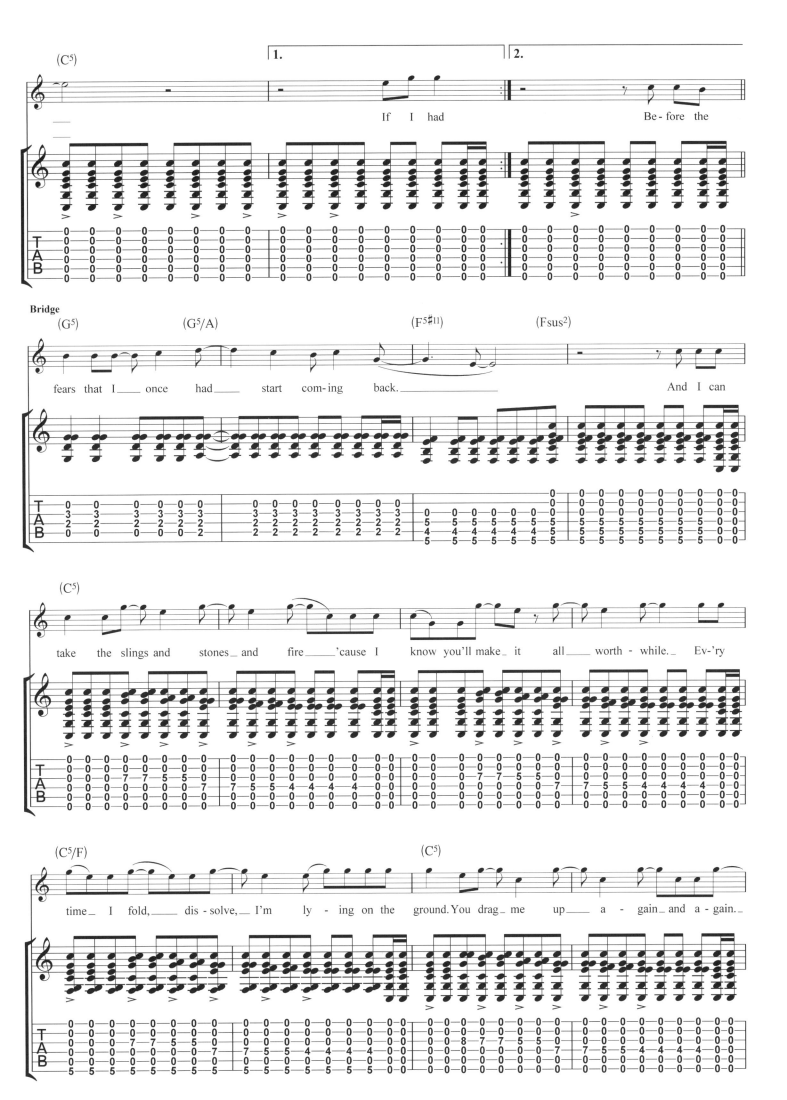

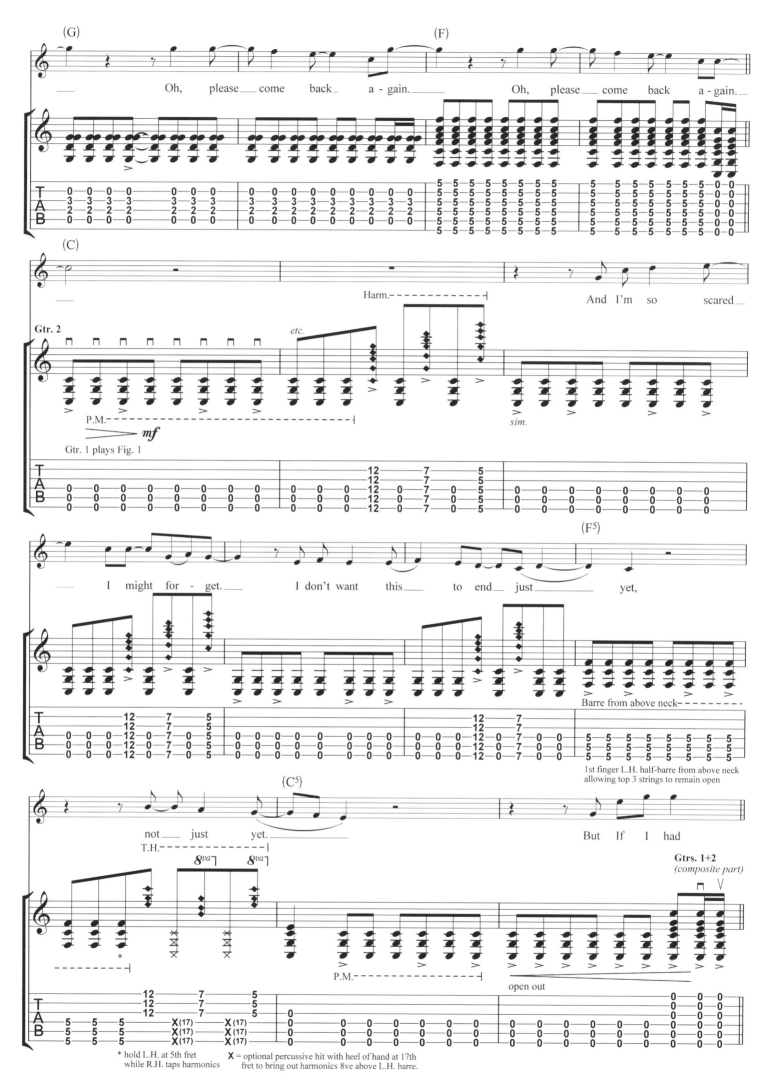

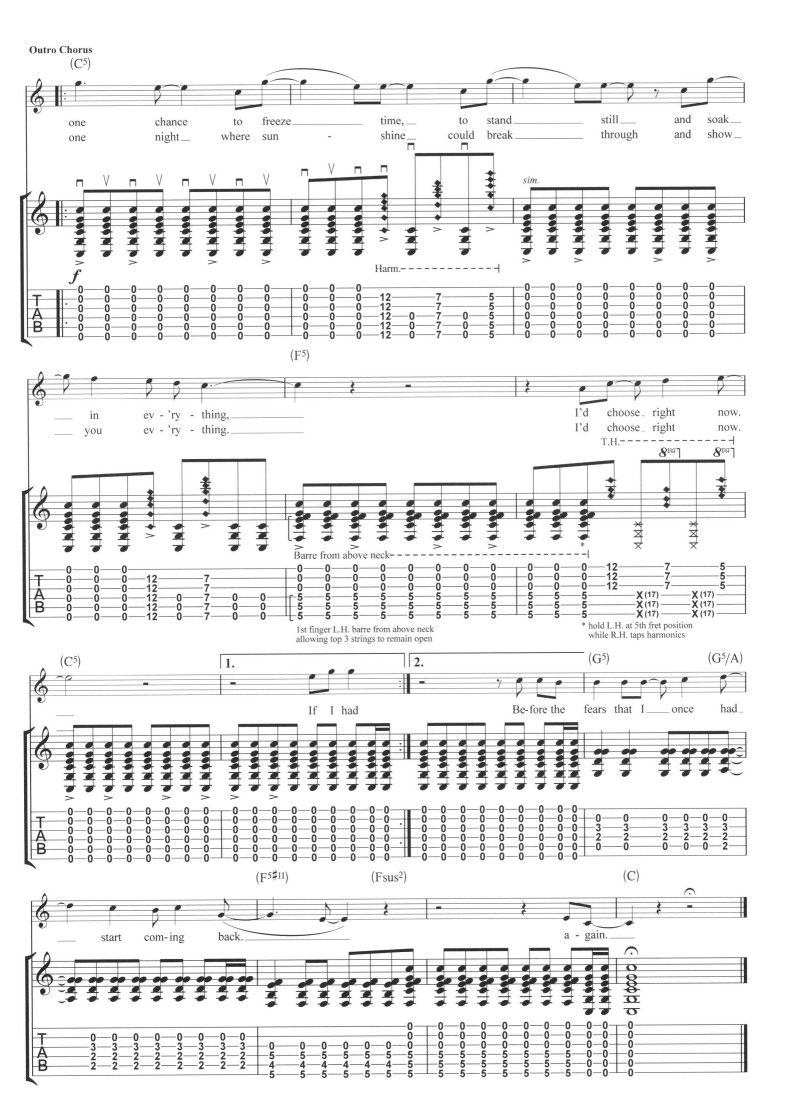

one   chance   to   freeze   time,   to   stand   still   and   soak
one   night   where   sun   -   shine   could   break   through   and   show

___ in ev-'ry-thing,___   I'd   choose   right   now.
___ you ev'ry-thing.___   I'd   choose   right   now.

Barre from above neck

1st finger L.H. barre from above neck
allowing top 3 strings to remain open

* hold L.H. at 5th fret position
while R.H. taps harmonics

If I had   Be-fore the   fears   that   I ___ once   had ___

___ start com-ing   back. ___   a - gain. ___

resin on my heart strings

Words & Music by Newton Faulkner

Tuning
6 = E	3 = G
5 = A	2 = B
4 = D	1 = E

To match the recording, tune guitar down a semitone

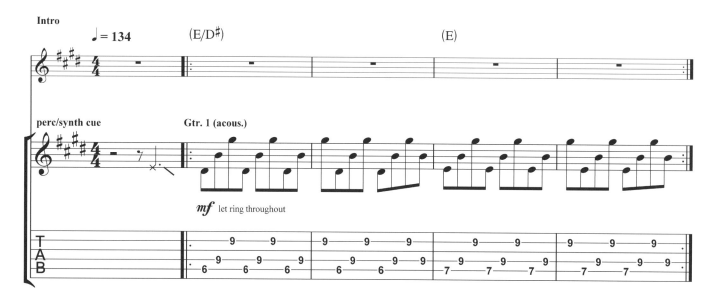

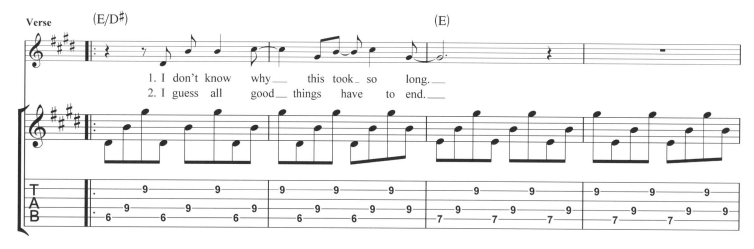

1. I don't know why___ this took_ so long.___
2. I guess all good___ things have to end.___

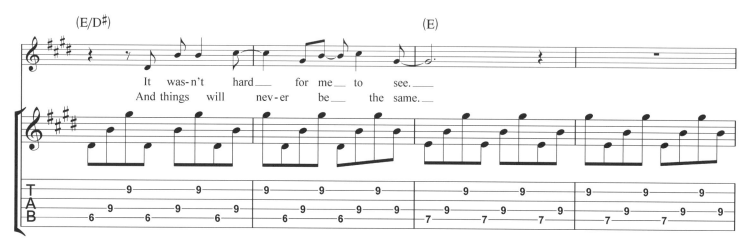

It was-n't hard___ for me_ to see.___
And things will nev-er be___ the same.___

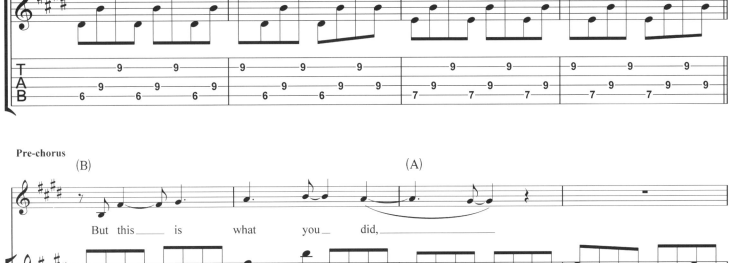

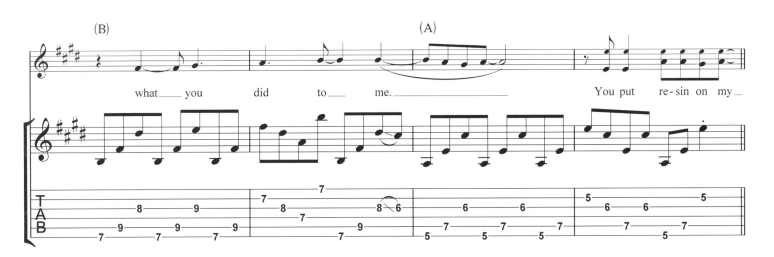

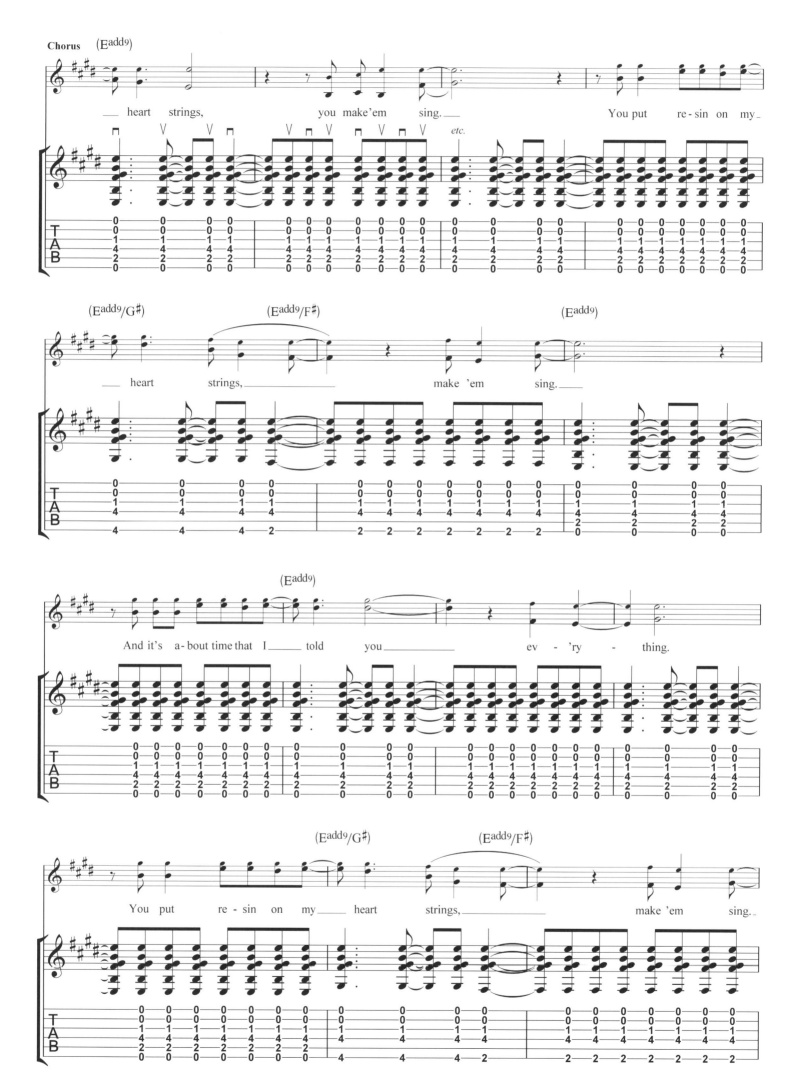

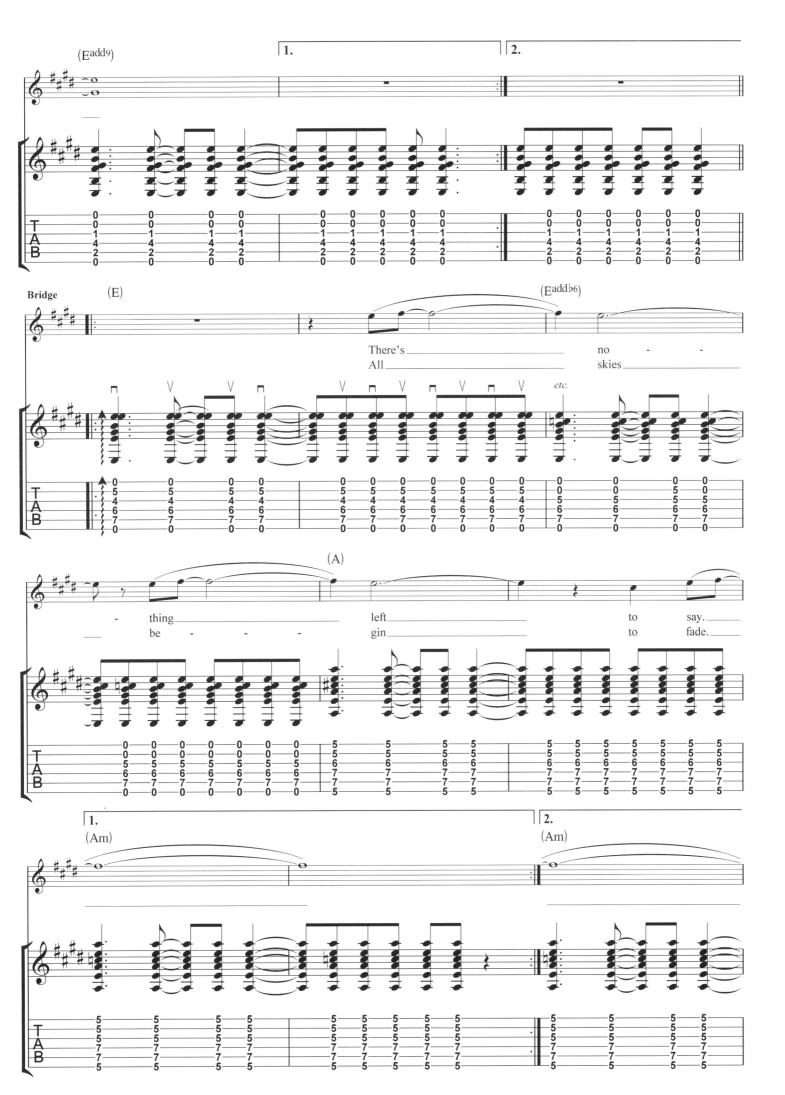

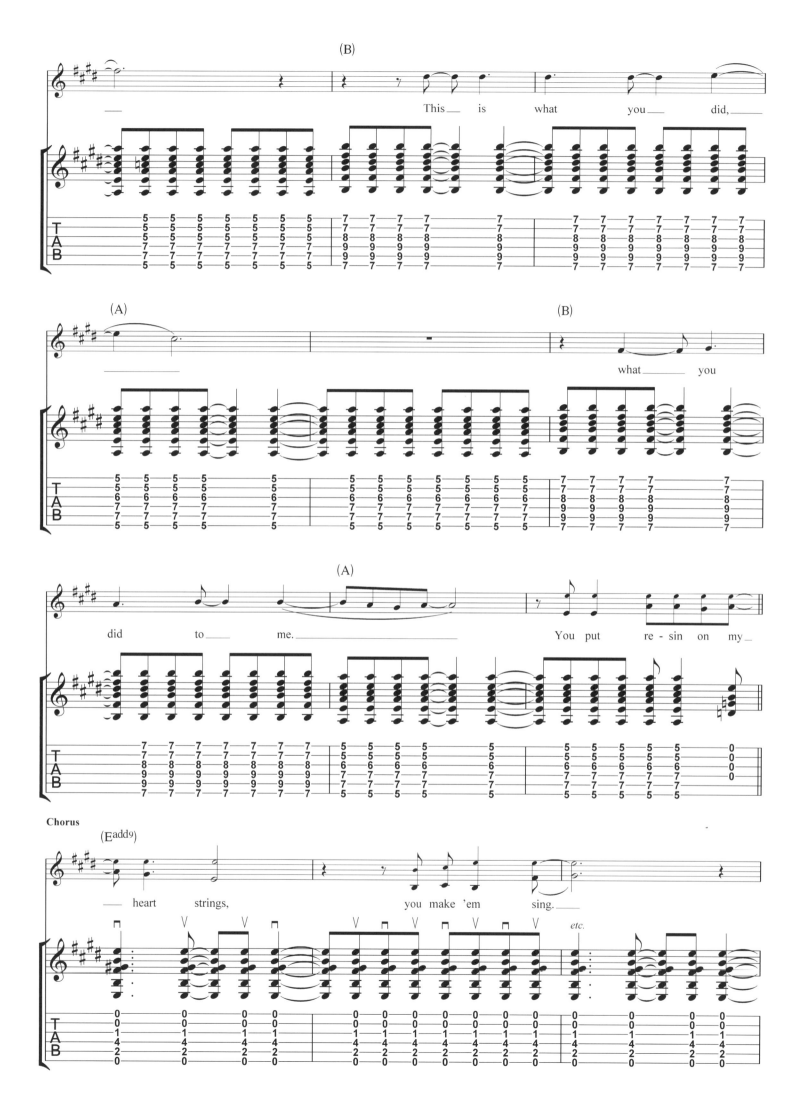

32

lipstick jungle

Words & Music by Newton Faulkner & Dee Adam

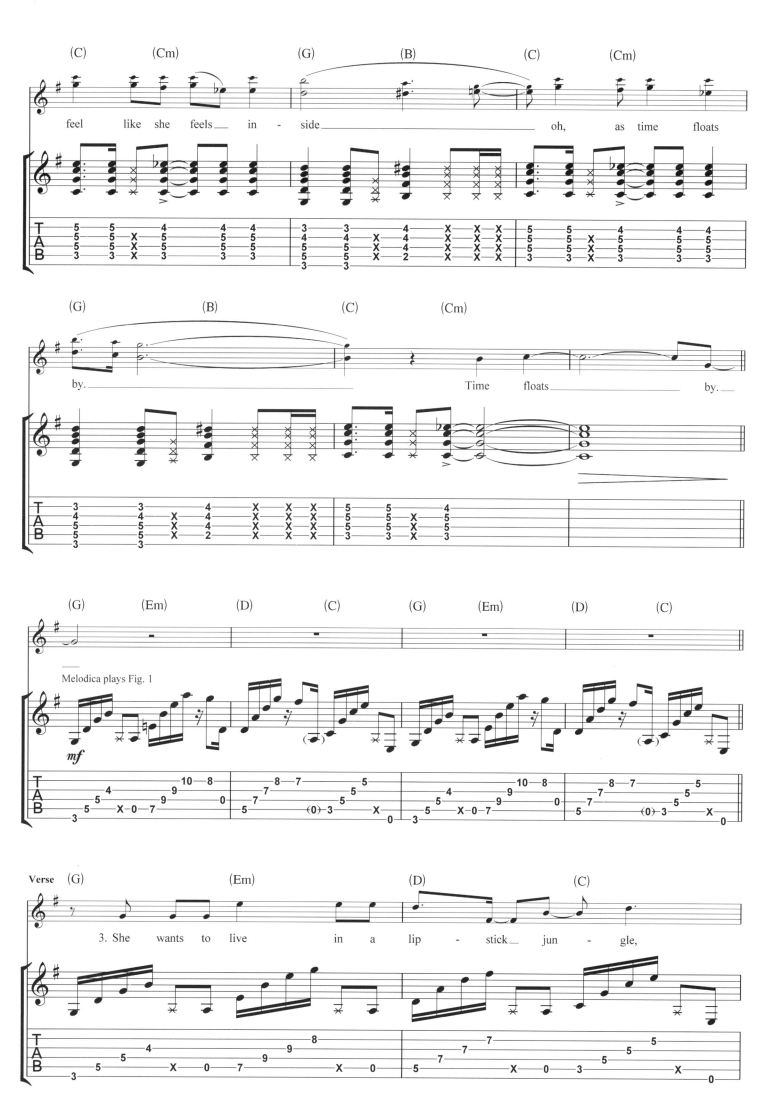

been thinking about it

Words & Music by Newton Faulkner

Tuning
6 = D 3 = G
5 = G 2 = A
4 = D 1 = D

To match recording, tune guitar down a semitone

Intro

♩ = 126

Gtr. 1 (acous.)

Verse

I was lost, lost at sea, I'd grab the flag and
(2.) I like you and you like me, why the hell are we

42

43

let's get together

Words & Music by Newton Faulkner & Toby Faulkner

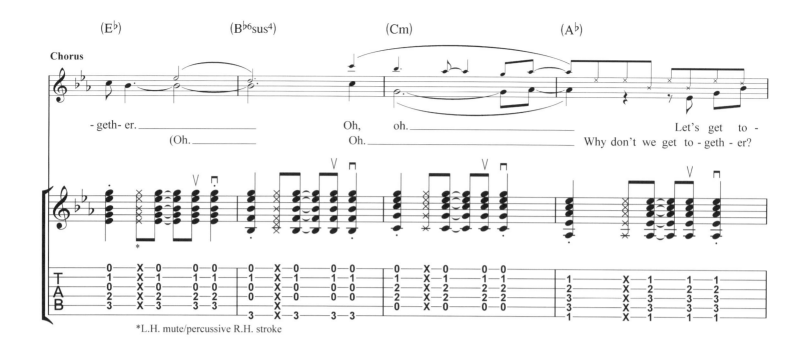

*L.H. mute/percussive R.H. stroke

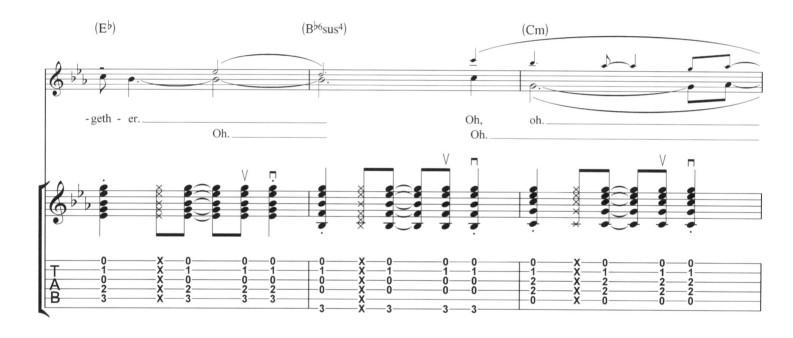

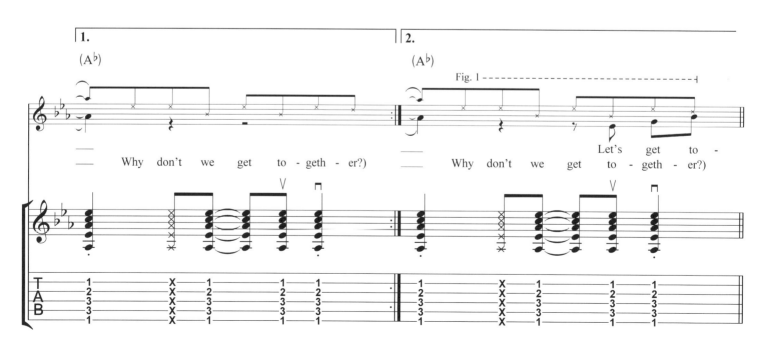

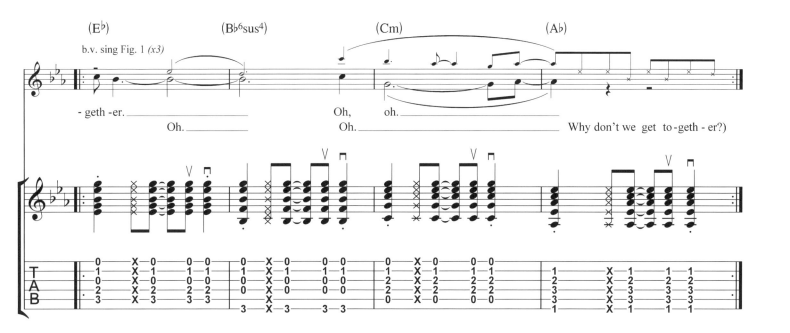

Breakdown

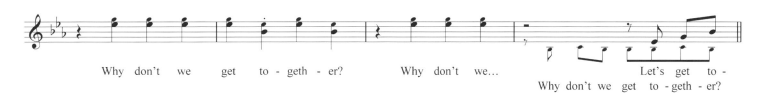

Outro-chorus

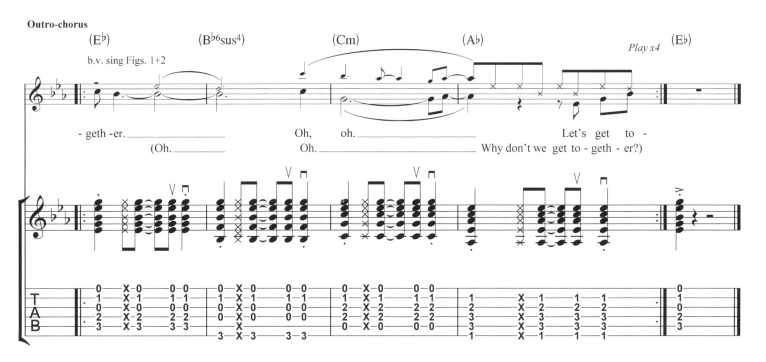

she's got the time 2 (interlude)

Words & Music by Newton Faulkner & Toby Faulkner

To match recording, tune guitar down a semitone

Verse lyrics:

1. Driving down the street, there's a girl on the corner in the sunshine, I'm gonna wind down the window, say "Hey, hi, how's it going?" How's she gonna take it, God knows.

2. Flying to L.A. with my sound man, bass man, drum man, I'm tired, wanna go to bed man, twenty guitars, a metal plate in my arm, oh God no.

3. Sipping on a drink backstage after party, guess the champagne's O.K., try to be friendly, I say "Hey do you want a canape?" She says "NO!"

won't let go

Words & Music by Newton Faulkner & Keigo Oyamada

Tuning	
6 = C	3 = G
5 = G	2 = A
4 = D	1 = E

To match recording tune guitar down a further semitone

♩ = 158

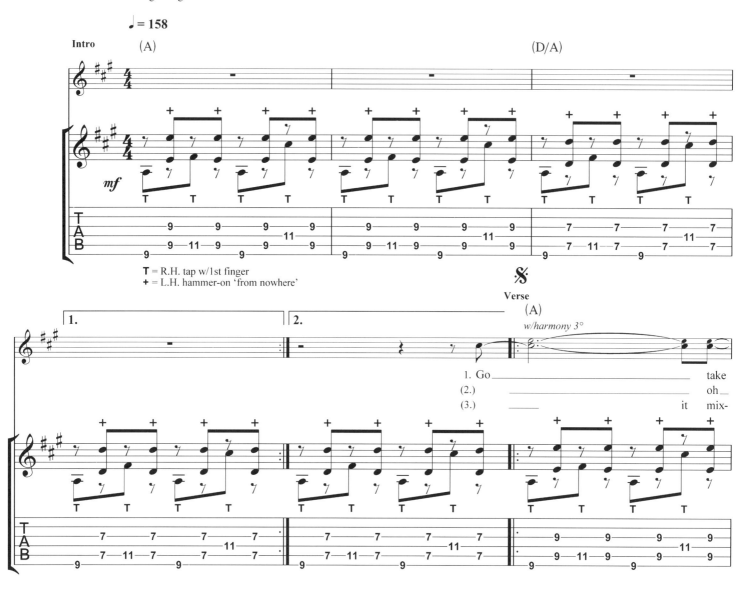

T = R.H. tap w/1st finger
+ = L.H. hammer-on 'from nowhere'

53

Time moves slow - ly on your own, you're

think - ing for your - self it's time. You won't let go

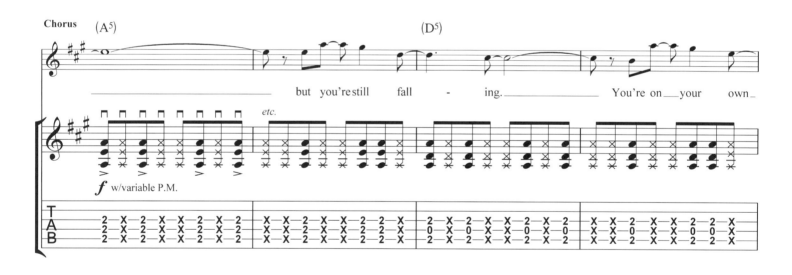

Chorus

but you're still fall - ing. You're on your own

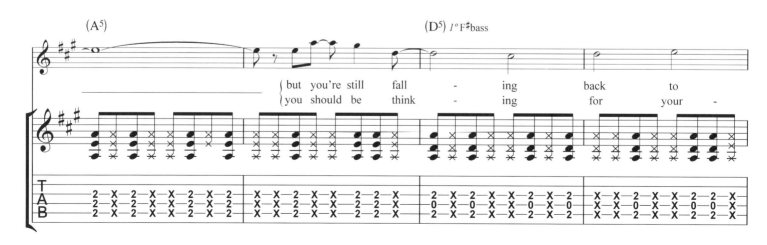

but you're still fall - ing back to

you should be think - ing for your -

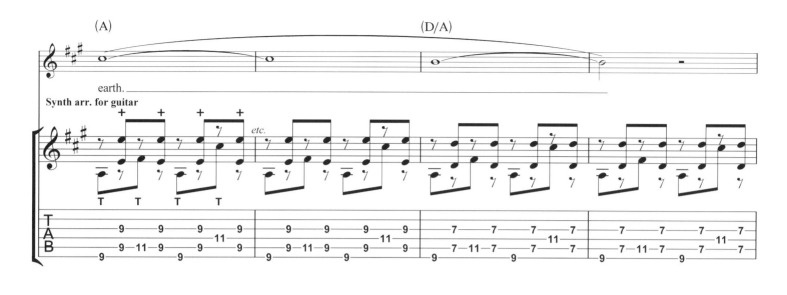

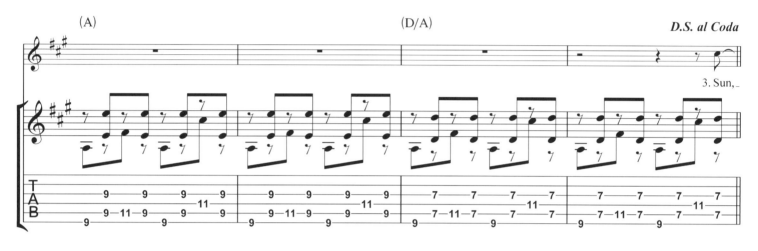

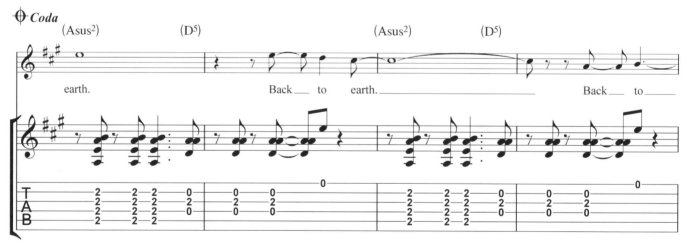

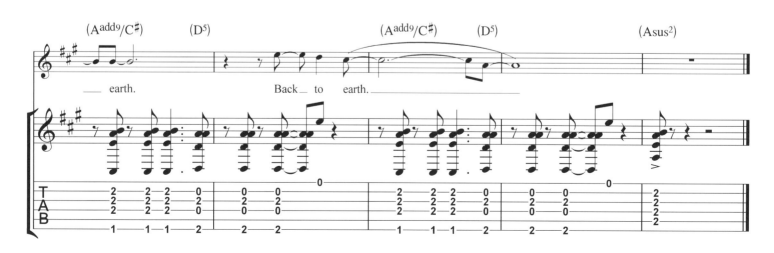

first time

Words & Music by Newton Faulkner & Adam Argyle

Tuning
6 = C	3 = G
5 = G	2 = A
4 = D	1 = D

Capo 8th fret

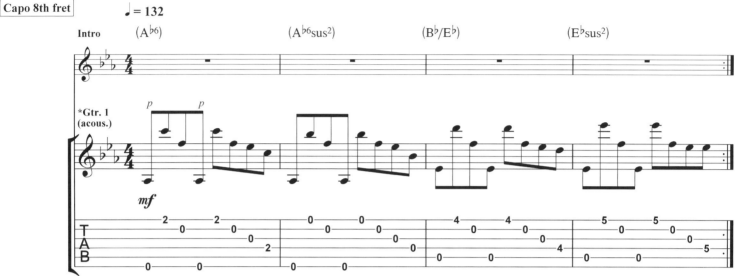

*On the album this song was played on Baritone guitar (tuned A♭ E♭ B♭ E♭ F B♭). It is arranged here for standard acoustic.
Tab 0 = Capo 8th fret

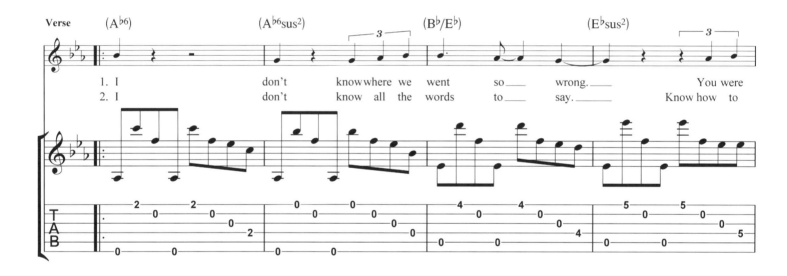

1. I don't know where we went so wrong. You were
2. I don't know all the words to say. Know how to

right there but some-how my friend had gone. O-kay, we got
please you, not how to re - lieve your pain. One day we'll look

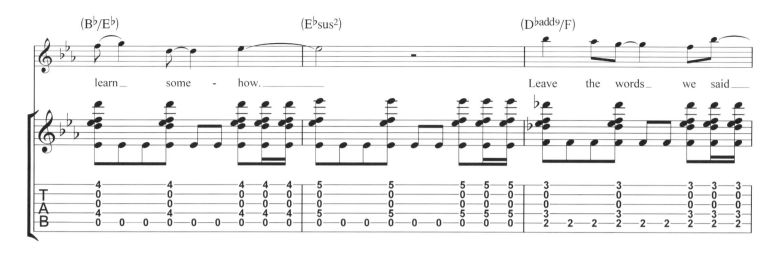

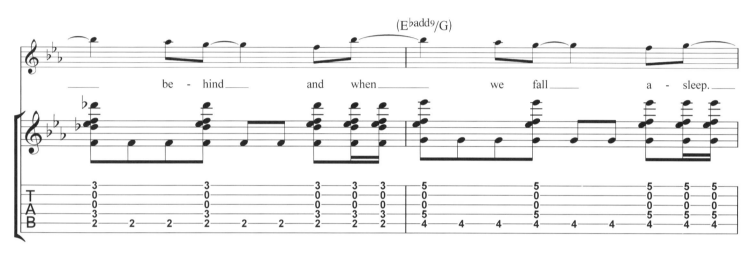

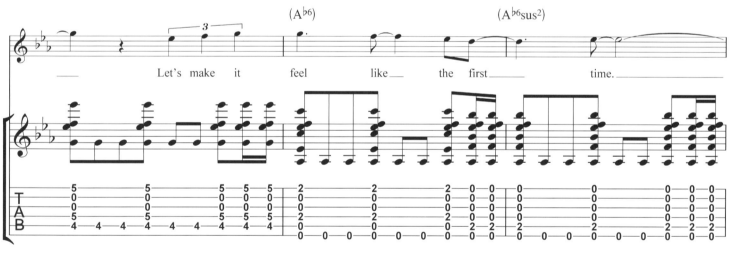

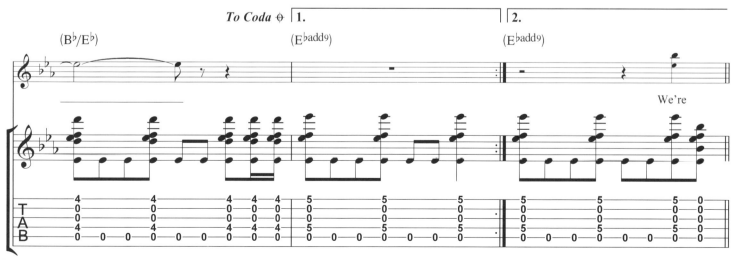

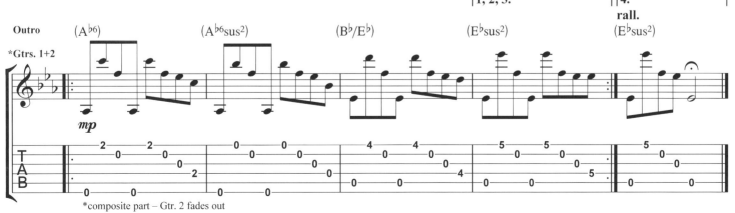

over and out

Words & Music by Newton Faulkner, Craigie Dodds & Ben Earle

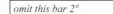

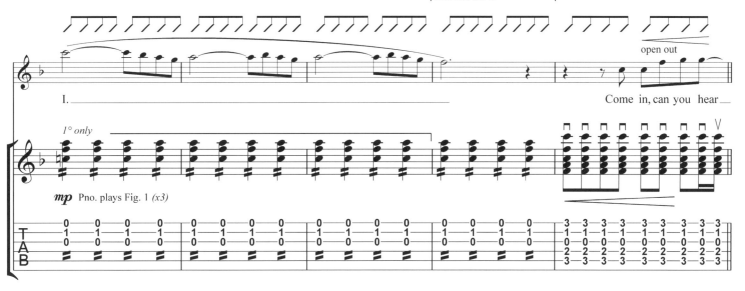

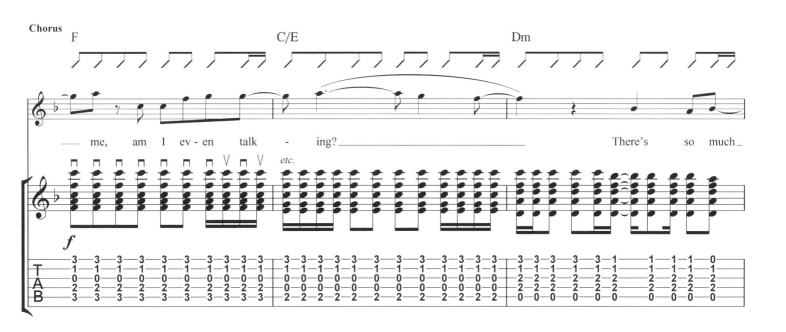

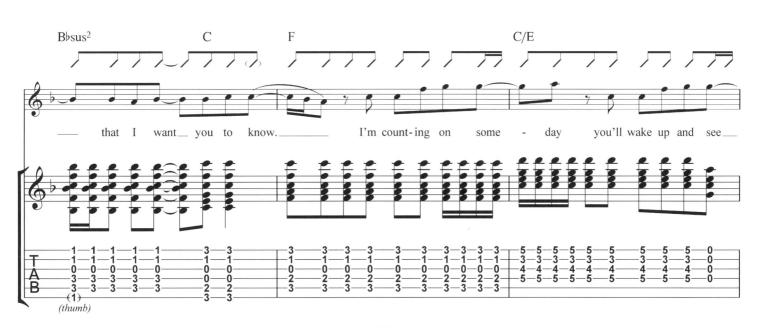

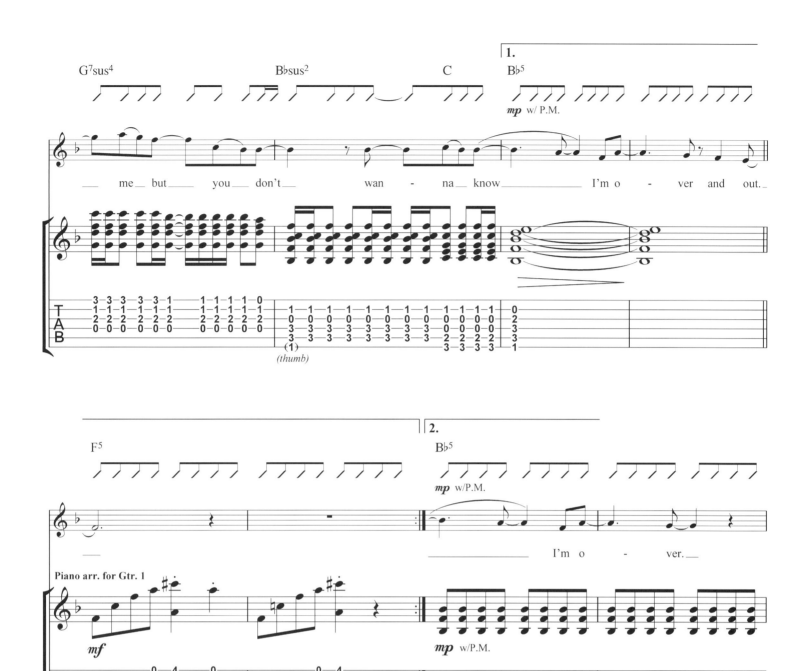

____ me__ but__ you__ don't__ wan - na_ know____ I'm o - ver and out._

____ I'm o - ver.__

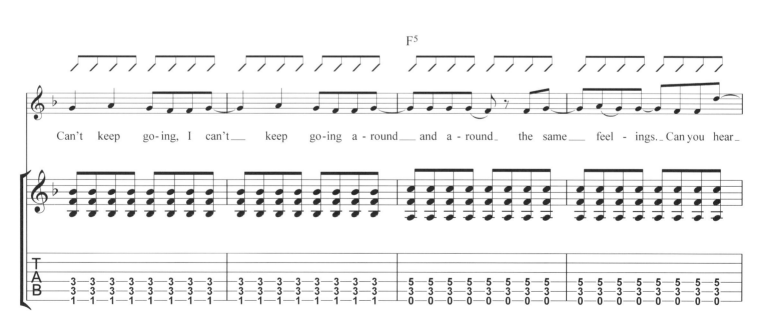

Can't keep go-ing, I can't__ keep go-ing a - round__ and a - round_ the same__ feel - ings. Can you hear__

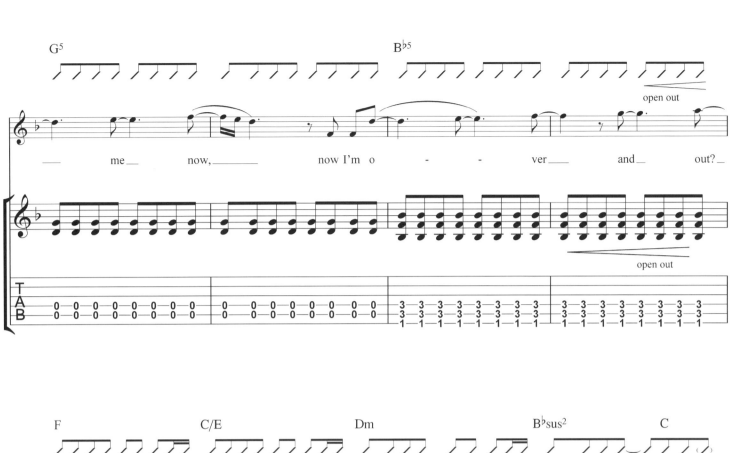

me ___ now, _____ now I'm o - - ver ___ and ___ out? ___

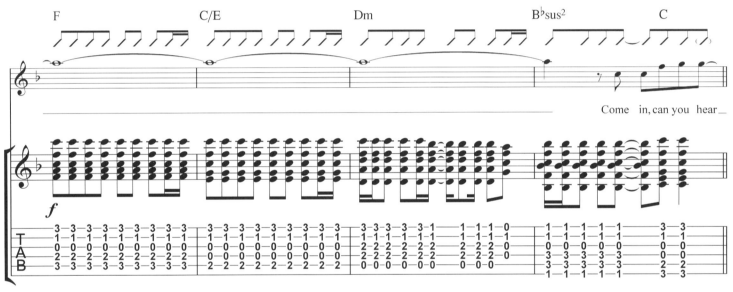

Come in, can you hear ___

Outro chorus

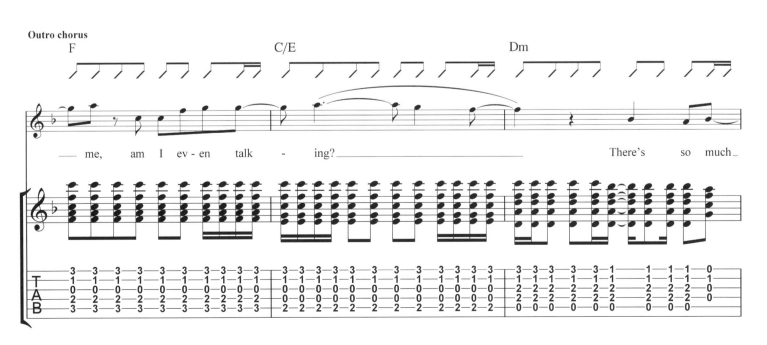

___ me, am I ev - en talk - ing? _____ There's so much ___

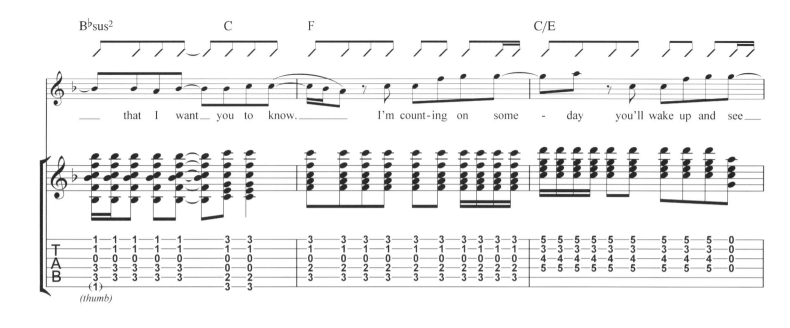

that I want you to know. I'm count-ing on some - day you'll wake up and see

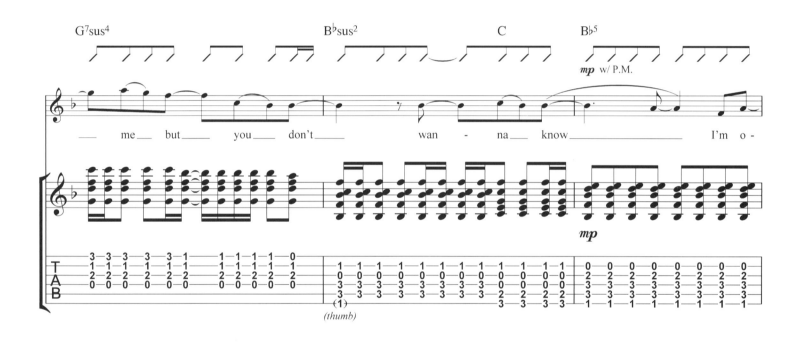

me but you don't wan - na know I'm o-

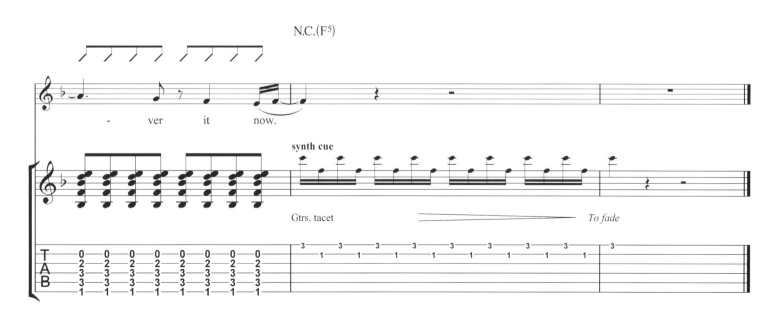

- ver it now.

cheltenham (interlude)

Tuning	
6 = D	3 = G
5 = A	2 = A
4 = D	1 = D

To match the recording, use a Capo, 1st fret

♩ = 160

Gtr. 1 (acous. - guitarlele)

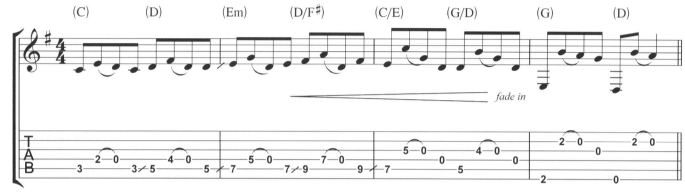

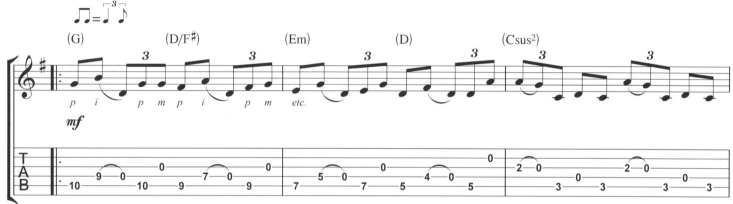

p = thumb *i* = index *m* = middle

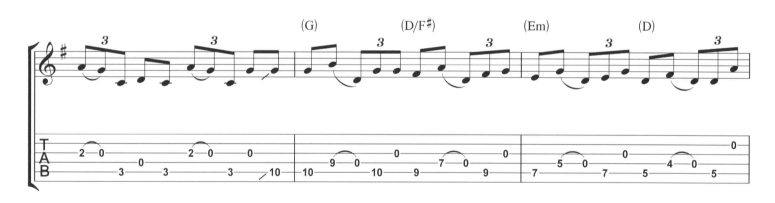

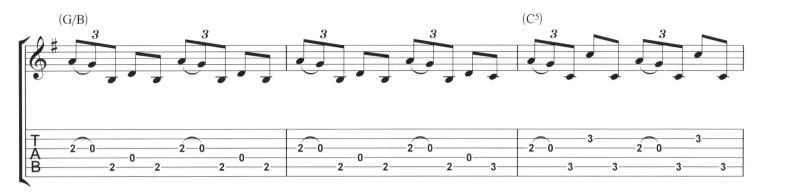

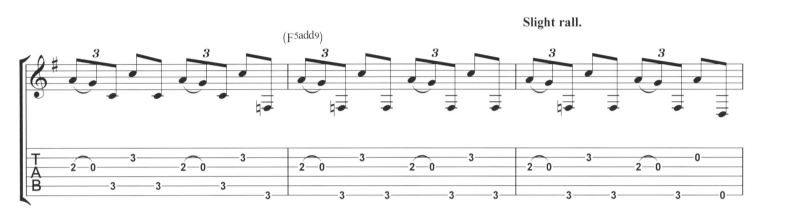

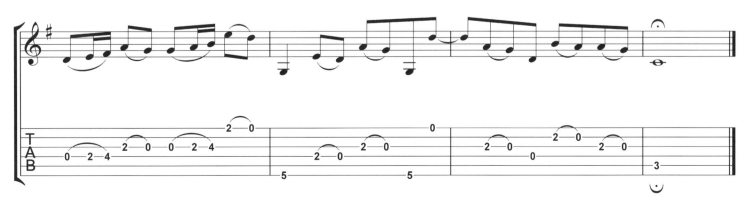

so much

Words & Music by Newton Faulkner

Tuning	
6 = E	3 = G
5 = A	2 = B
4 = D	1 = E

To match the recording tune guitar down a semitone

Intro ♩ = 104

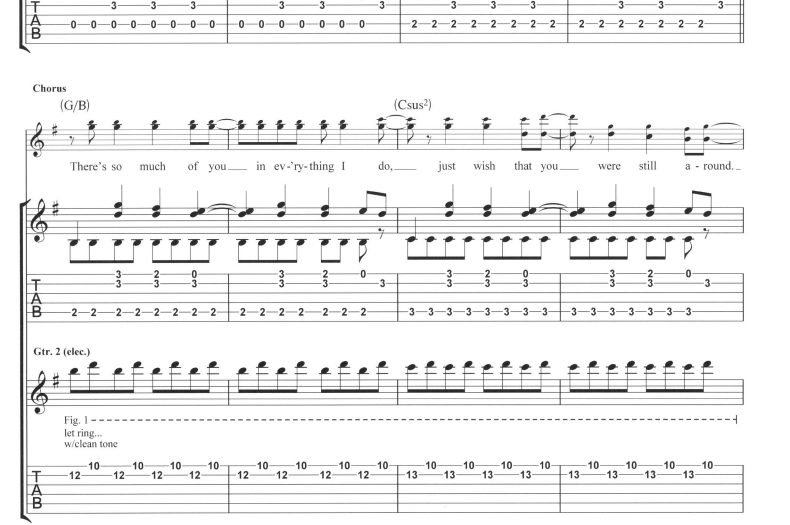

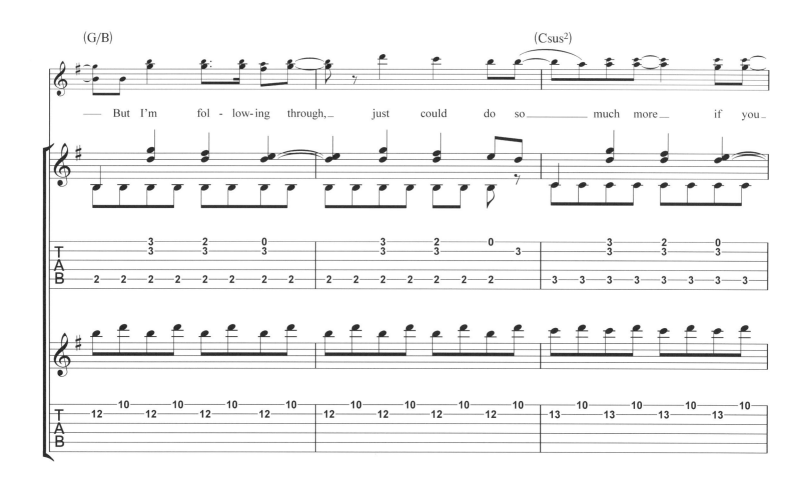

— But I'm fol - low-ing through, just could do so much more if you

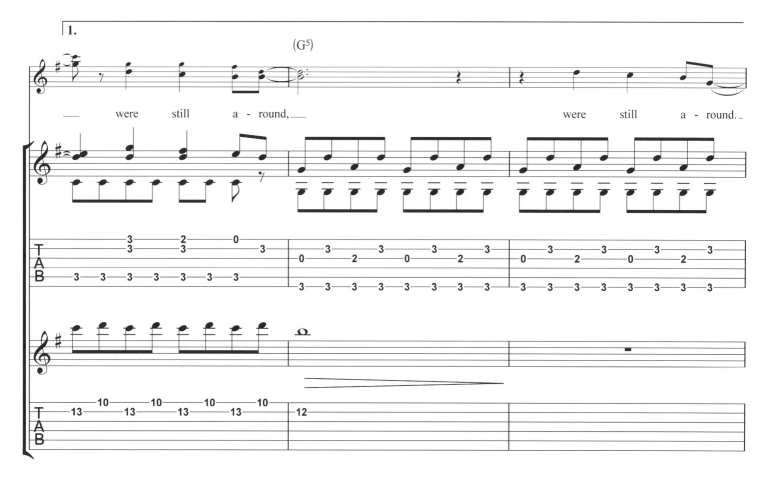

1.

— were still a - round, were still a - round.

74

This Town

Words & Music by Newton Faulkner & Dee Adam

Percussive notation:

X = L.H. mute/percussive R.H. stroke

T = tap at 12th fret with flat of index finger to get mix of harmonics and open string sound

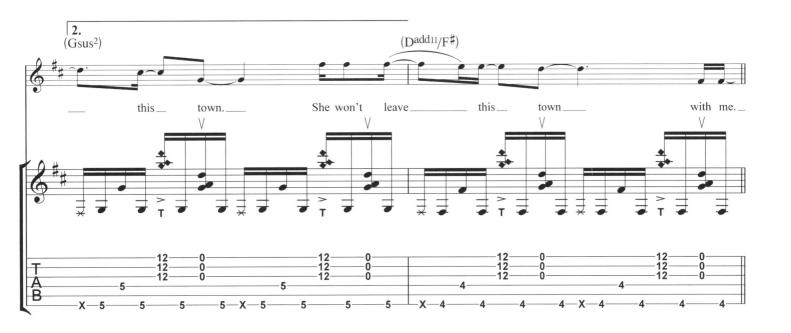

2.
(Gsus²) (Dadd11/F#)

this town. She won't leave this town with me.

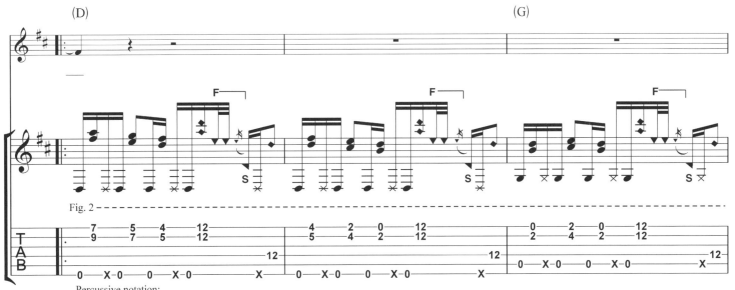

(D) (G)

Fig. 2

Percussive notation:
x = L.H. mute/percussive R.H. stroke
F = percussive hit (*rasqueado*) with R.H. fingers below sound-hole
S = L.H. hit on lower left side of guitar

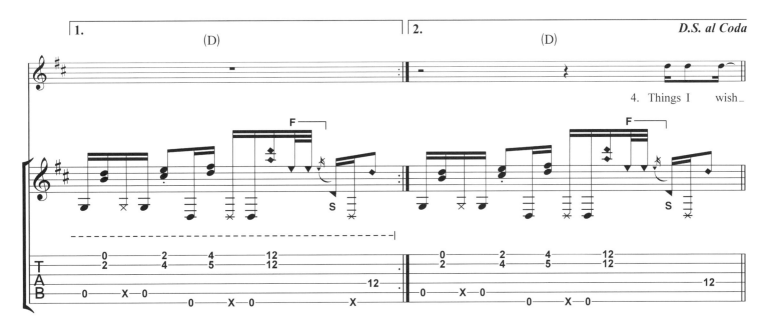

1. (D) **2.** (D) ***D.S. al Coda***

4. Things I wish

⊕ *Coda*

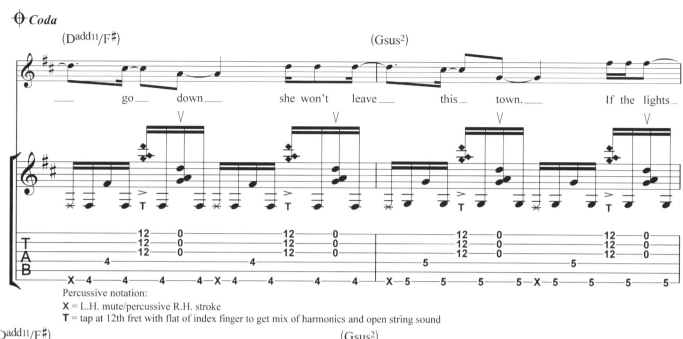

Percussive notation:

X = L.H. mute/percussive R.H. stroke

T = tap at 12th fret with flat of index finger to get mix of harmonics and open string sound

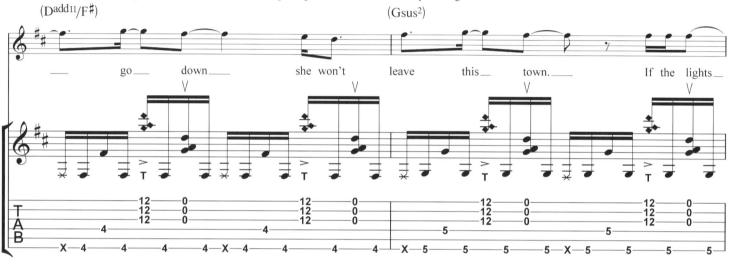

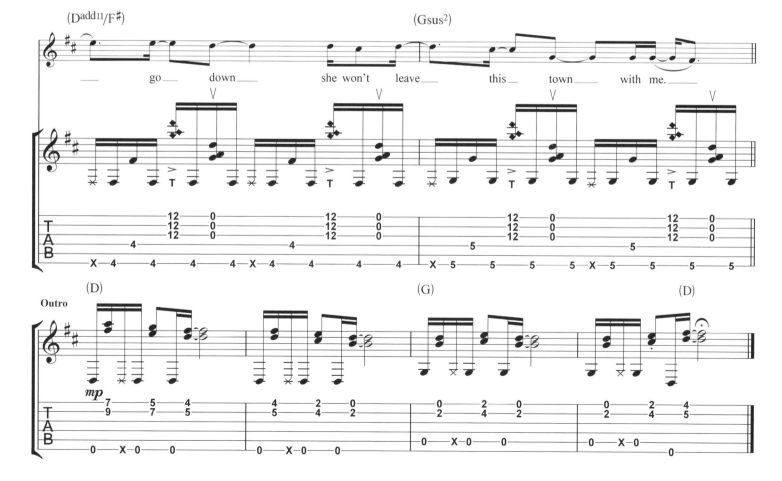

i'm not giving up yet

Words & Music by Newton Faulkner

Tuning
6 = D   3 = F♯
5 = A   2 = A
4 = D   1 = D

To match recording tune guitar down a semitone

Intro

♩ = 148

**Gtr. 1
(acous.)**

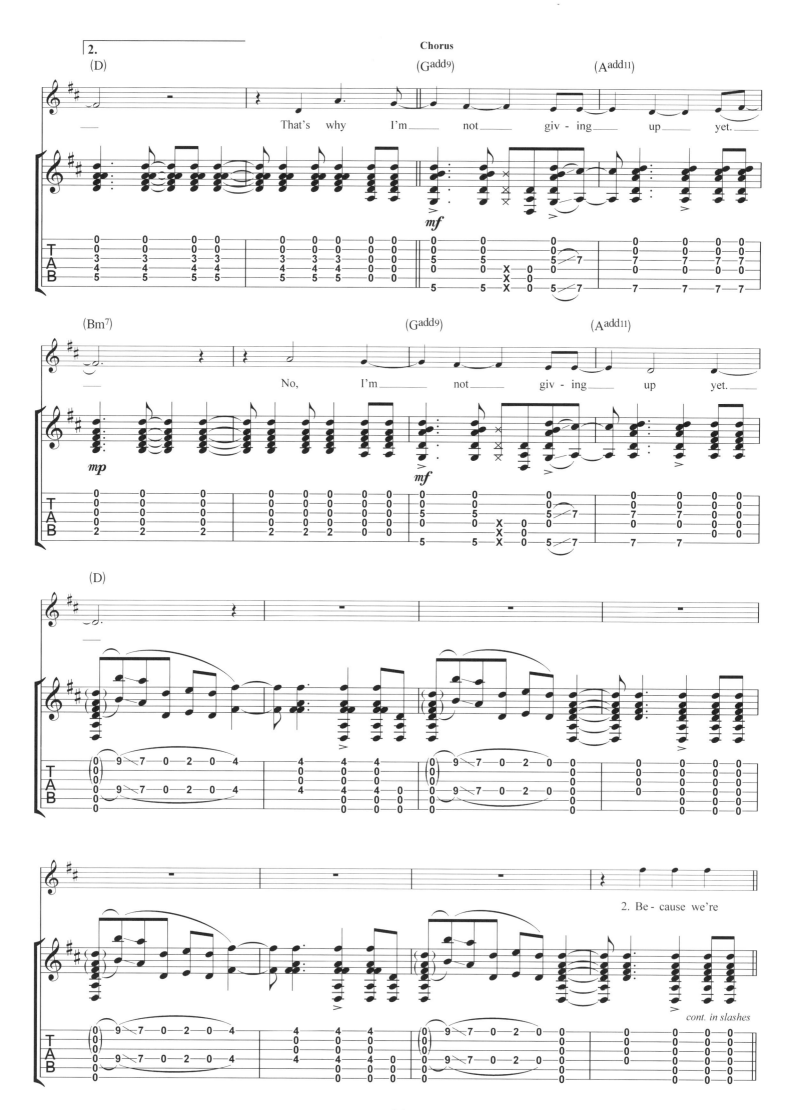

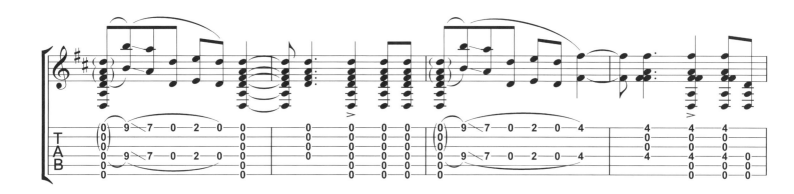

Bridge

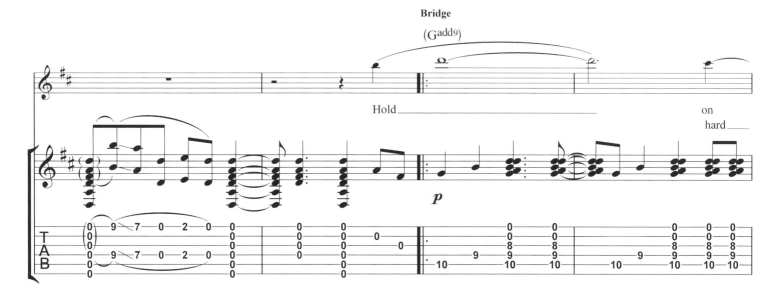

Hold_____ on hard____

to a- -ny truth_____ that_____ you find.____

____ these days____ to tell____ right from wrong and wrong

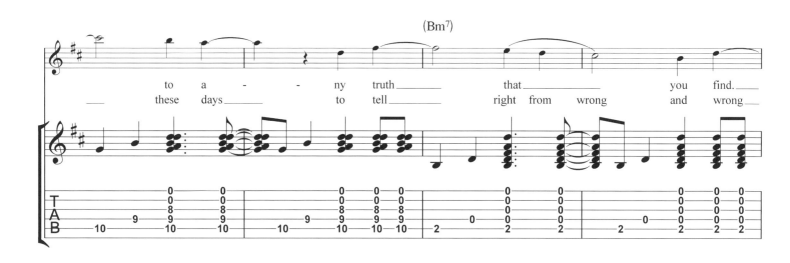

1. **2.**

It's so____ ____ from right. But I'm

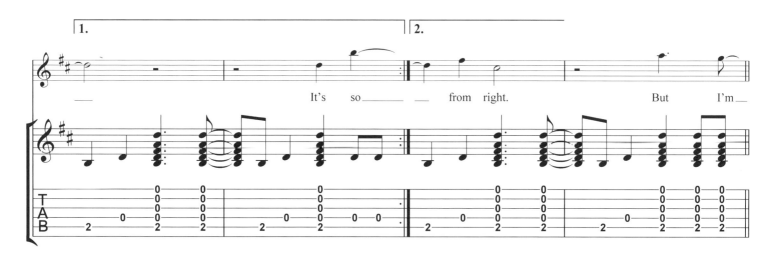